Our influence on the Earth

Graham Hill

Conservation workers rebuilding a dry stone wall between National Trust property and farmland in the Gower Peninsula, Wales

Contents

Activities

1 Our needs

Look at figure 1 below. It shows how we need food, water, air and warmth in order to live.

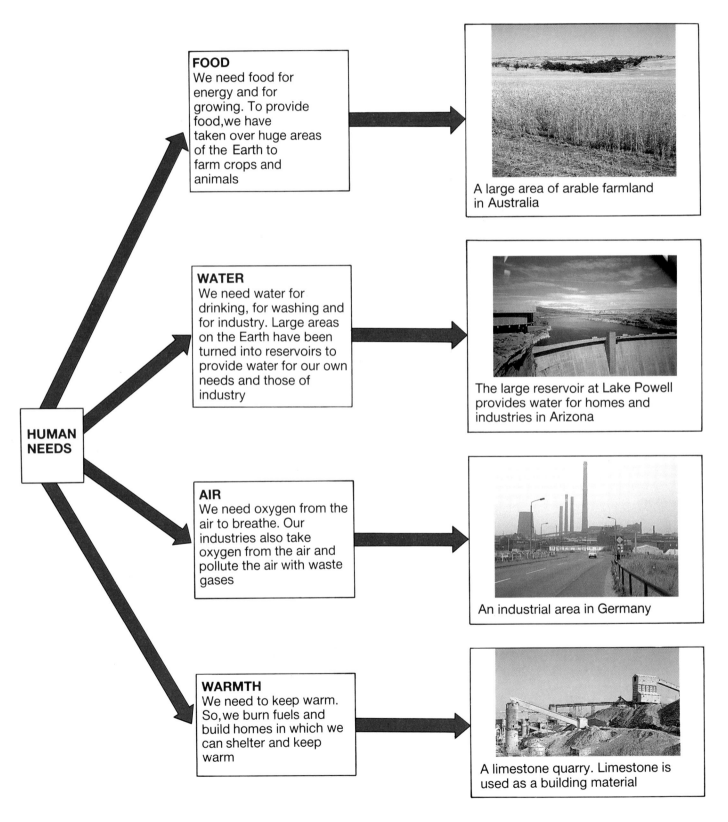

FOOD
We need food for energy and for growing. To provide food, we have taken over huge areas of the Earth to farm crops and animals

A large area of arable farmland in Australia

WATER
We need water for drinking, for washing and for industry. Large areas on the Earth have been turned into reservoirs to provide water for our own needs and those of industry

The large reservoir at Lake Powell provides water for homes and industries in Arizona

HUMAN NEEDS

AIR
We need oxygen from the air to breathe. Our industries also take oxygen from the air and pollute the air with waste gases

An industrial area in Germany

WARMTH
We need to keep warm. So, we burn fuels and build homes in which we can shelter and keep warm

A limestone quarry. Limestone is used as a building material

Figure 1 We all need food, water, air and warmth

We all need food, water, air and warmth. In trying to provide these for everyone, we have changed the Earth's surface for ever. Large areas of land have been taken over for farming. In some areas, huge forests have been cut down to provide wood for fuel and create space for farming. Quarries and mines have been developed to obtain valuable materials from the Earth. These materials and resources have been used to build homes and motorways where there was once countryside.

We have also caused changes in the atmosphere and changes in the rivers, lakes and oceans around the Earth. Valleys have been dammed and flooded to provide water for crops, industries and homes. At the same time, we have used up valuable resources from the Earth and produced waste materials which pollute our air, our water and our land.

If the changes that we make in our environment are too great, some kinds of animals and plants may die out (become extinct).

Things to do

1 Look at the photos below. Describe the changes which have taken place in the area photographed between 1890 and 1992.

2 Look at figure 1 again.
a) Make a list of ten important advantages that we have gained in trying to provide food, water, air and warmth for everyone.
b) Make a list of ten disadvantages that have resulted from trying to provide food, water, air and warmth for everyone.
c) Why do you think that people are now more concerned about resources than they were 50 years ago?

3 Get into a group with 2 or 3 others. Discuss ways in which your school grounds might be improved for the environment. Write a short report of your discussion for your class.

4 Suppose a company wants to build a large leisure complex in the area near your school.
a) What benefits do you think this might bring to the area?
b) What problems do you think this might create?

5 At one time, ospreys almost died out in Britain. Since 1980, they have increased in number. There are now more than 60 nesting pairs. Find out more about ospreys in Britain.
a) Why did they almost die out?
b) What has been done to help their numbers increase in recent years?

2 Concrete or countryside

Everyday our factories and industries produce millions of tonnes of important man-made materials. These include metals, fuels, fertilisers and plastics. The first stage in making most of these products involves mining or quarrying. So, we drill and dig and quarry for raw materials like oil and copper ore.

Although mining and manufacture give us useful products, they also cause problems.

■ They spoil the countryside and our towns and villages with ugly concrete buildings, open-cast mines and huge pylons.

■ They produce waste products which pollute rivers, land and air. This pollution harms the environment.

■ They use raw materials like oil and metal ores which are scarce.

Although mines and industrial sites can damage the environment, these photos show how an area can be restored for leisure activities. A gravel pit (left) can be flooded and used for sailing (right).

Conserve and recycle

Today there are 5000 million people on the Earth. By the year 2000, the world's population will be about 7000 million. *More* people need *more* food, *more* water, *more* raw materials and *more* land. But, we know that the Earth's resources cannot last forever. This has led to important changes in the way we use valuable raw materials.

■ We have begun to use scarce resources, like oil and copper ore, more sparingly. We are also trying to use all raw materials more carefully and without waste. Conserving and saving the Earth's resources in this way is called **conservation**. You have probably heard of another form of conservation – conservation of the environment. In conserving the environment, we are trying to protect it and keep it in its natural state. This might mean protecting wildlife or not building roads.

■ One of the best ways to save and conserve raw materials is to re-use our waste. Discarded paper, plastics, glass, aluminium and steel are being collected to be used again. This is called **recycling**. Recycling can help us to save raw materials and prolong the life of limited resources like oil and natural gas. It can also save energy costs because it is cheaper to recycle materials like used glass than to make completely new glass.

Things to do

1 The six photos below show examples of conservation, recycling and pollution.

   a) Which photos show conservation?
   b) Describe what is happening in each of the conservation photos.
   c) Which photos show pollution?
   d) For each pollution photo,
      (i) what has caused the pollution,
      (ii) how do you think the pollution could be prevented?
   e) Which photos show recycling?
   f) Describe what is happening in each of the recycling photos.

2 Make a list of the things that you and your family throw into the dustbin each week.
   a) Which of these things could be recycled?
   b) Which of these things must be buried or burnt?
   c) Find out how you can help to recycle waste materials in your area.
   d) Make a poster for your area telling people how they can help locally to recycle waste.

3 Look at the photos on the opposite page. They show how a gravel pit can be restored. Write about a project in your area which has improved the environment. (Your local newspaper or library may help you with this question.)

3 What a waste!

Figure 1 The average contents of our dustbins

paper and card 28%

kitchen waste 27%

dust/ash 10%

glass 10%

metal 7%

cloth 7%

plastic 6%

other materials 5%

Rubbish and waste can be a problem. The biggest problem is how to get rid of it. Every year we throw away about 30 million tonnes of refuse. Someone has estimated that this rubbish is worth about £2500 000 000.

Figure 1 shows the average contents of our dustbins.

■ How does the waste from your family compare with the percentages in figure 1?

■ Which materials do you throw away more of?

■ Which materials do you throw away less of?

We can divide the rubbish we throw away into two types.

(i) Some waste, such as paper, wool, vegetables and food, will rot away (**decay**) if they are left for a time. These materials break down due to the action of bacteria. Because of this, they are described as **biodegradable**.

This fruit has rotted away over a period of a few days. It has been broken down (degraded) by the action of bacteria and fungi. Fruit, like other food, is biodegradable

(ii) Other kinds of waste, such as glass and plastics, will not rot away. They remain unchanged because bacteria cannot break them down or use them as food. Because of this, they are described as **non-biodegradable**. If we throw these materials away carelessly, they litter our towns and the countryside for years.

A scrap metal processing plant where iron and steel are separated for recycling

What do we do with waste?

Figure 2 shows the four most common ways in which we deal with waste. These are:

- land fill,
- recycling,
- incineration,
- making biogas.

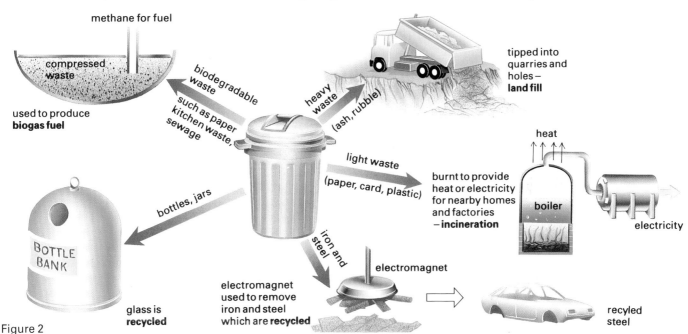

Figure 2

1 Look at the information in figure 1.
a) Draw a pie chart of the average contents of our dustbins.
b) In which type of waste would you put:
(i) old socks, (ii) dry bread, (iii) empty cans?
c) 'Other material' makes up 5% of our dustbin waste in figure 1. Give one example of rubbish that might be classified as 'other material'.
d) Which of the types of waste in figure 1 should we recycle?

2 Here are the contents of a rubbish bin:
several newspapers, two milk bottles, a wine bottle, seven milk bottle tops, some baking foil, three empty soup cans, two pairs of nylon tights, potato peelings, a cotton vest, some polythene sheeting, coal ash.
a) Which of these materials are biodegradable?
b) Which of these materials could be recycled?
c) Which of these materials should be buried or burnt?

3 Design an experiment to investigate whether waste food rots (degrades) faster:
a) at 40°C or 20°C,
b) when it is wet or dry.

In 1273, an attempt was made to ban the burning of coal in London. Even then, people knew that smoke from fires was polluting the air.

Nearly 400 years later in 1661, John Evelyn wrote a book about the 'smoke of London'. Evelyn warned people about the dangers of polluting the air with smoke from coal fires.

In spite of these warnings, smoke pollution in London went from bad to worse. It caused bronchitis and other lung diseases. In 1952, over 4000 people died from **smog** in London. Smog is a mixture of smoke and fog.

The smog of Los Angeles is notorious. The photo above was taken at 11 a.m.

This policeman is wearing a mask to protect himself from the smoke and fog (smog) in London in 1953.

Because of these disasters, parliament passed special laws in 1956, 1968 and 1974 to cut down air pollution. In 1956, the **Clean Air Act** made it illegal to pollute the air with soot and smoke from factories and homes. Local authorities were given the power to set up Smoke Control Areas (**Smokeless Zones**). In these areas, people must use gas, electricity or smokeless fuels such as coke or anthracite. By 1978, the amount of smoke put into our atmosphere was reduced to about one sixth.

One of these lungs came from a Londoner in the 1950s. The other was from a person who lived in the country. Which is which? Why do the lungs differ in size and colour?

Detecting pollution

In any area there are clues which indicate the level of air pollution.
You can see some of these clues in the photos below.

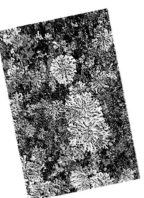

Brown and orange lichens cannot survive in highly polluted areas but some grey-green lichens are able to grow in polluted regions.

Roses are attacked by a common virus which causes black spots on the leaves if the air is clean. In polluted areas, this virus cannot survive so there are no black spots on the rose leaves.

Evidence of water pollution below the sluice gates on the River Avon in Tewkesbury. Not all water pollution is so obvious.

Things to do

1 Fog occurs when water vapour condenses to form droplets of water in the air.

   a) What causes the water vapour to condense?

   b) At what time of day is fog most likely to form?

   c) At what time of year is fog most likely to form?

   d) At what time of year is smoke most likely to pollute the air the most?

   e) Why is smoke and fog pollution called 'smog'?

2 a) What was the main cause of smoke pollution in London during the 1950s?

   b) What problems did this smoke pollution cause?

   c) What steps were taken in the 1950s to reduce the smoke pollution in London?

   d) Find out about present-day smog problems such as those in Los Angeles.

3 Manjit and Alan decided to compare the quantity of smoke particles in the air at home and at school. They have a small electric air pump, some filter paper, cotton wool and normal laboratory equipment.

   a) Draw a well-labelled diagram of the apparatus they could use.

   b) Describe what they should do.

   c) List the measurements they should make.

4 Look at the section headed *Detecting pollution*. Carry out a survey on pollution in your area. Write a report of your survey.

In Tokyo, the traffic police wear gas masks because of the pollution from car exhausts

Most air pollution is caused by burning fuels. The problems are therefore worst in industrial areas where there are factories and power stations. Fuels like coal, oil and natural gas contain carbon. If the fuel burns completely, all this carbon reacts with oxygen in the air to form **carbon dioxide**. If there is not much air available, the carbon forms **soot** and **smoke** or it may form **carbon monoxide**. Carbon monoxide is very poisonous.

Some fuels, like coal and coke, contain small amounts of sulphur. When these fuels burn, **sulphur dioxide** is produced.

$$\text{sulphur in fuel} + \text{oxygen in air} \rightarrow \text{sulphur dioxide}$$

Sulphur dioxide is a colourless, choking gas. It makes us cough, it causes our eyes to water and it attacks our lungs. When it rains, the sulphur dioxide reacts with the water to form an acid solution containing sulphurous acid and sulphuric acid.

$$\text{sulphur dioxide} + \text{water} \rightarrow \text{sulphurous acid}$$

This acid solution in rain water is called **acid rain** (figure 1). Acid rain harms plants, it stunts the growth of trees and it even attacks stone buildings.

Acid rain has damaged this stone monument in Ilam village, Derbyshire

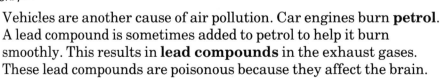

This lake looks clear and blue because it has been poisoned by acid rain

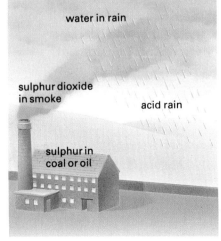

water in rain

sulphur dioxide in smoke

acid rain

sulphur in coal or oil

Figure 1

Vehicles are another cause of air pollution. Car engines burn **petrol**. A lead compound is sometimes added to petrol to help it burn smoothly. This results in **lead compounds** in the exhaust gases. These lead compounds are poisonous because they affect the brain.

Car engines need air to burn petrol. When the petrol burns in the engine, nitrogen and oxygen combine to form **nitrogen dioxide**. This is an acidic gas which causes further air pollution. It irritates our eyes and lungs like sulphur dioxide (figure 2).

Preventing pollution

There are ways of preventing pollution, but they all cost money.

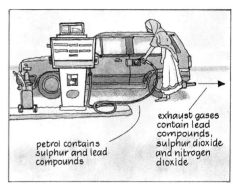

Figure 2

1 Low sulphur fuels

Oil refineries can produce oil that is low in sulphur. Most coal can be cleaned to reduce the sulphur content before it is burnt. These measures increase the cost of the fuel.

2 Unleaded petrol

Car engines have been designed to use unleaded petrol. Unleaded petrol is more expensive to produce than leaded petrol. In the last few years, the Government has reduced the tax on unleaded petrol so that, overall, it is now cheaper than leaded petrol.

3 Smokeless fuels

Smokeless fuels must be used in smoke control areas ('smokeless zones'). Since 1956, Parliament has passed several laws to reduce the soot and smoke from chimneys and car exhausts.

4 Scrubbing

The waste gases from factories and power stations using coal and oil are possibly the worst cause of acid rain. If these gases are passed through an alkaline solution of lime, 95% of the acidic gases can be removed. This process adds to costs.

The Houses of Parliament before and after the soot was cleaned from their stonework

Things to do

1 Which of these words fill the numbered gaps in the paragraph below?

air, blood, brain, carbon dioxide, carbon monoxide, closed, garage, open, oxygen, soil, stadium

'Carbon monoxide reacts with a substance in the ___(1)___ called haemoglobin. This stops the haemoglobin carrying ___(2)___ to the ___(3)___ and other parts of our bodies. It is dangerous to run a car engine in a ___(4)___ with the doors ___(5)___ because lack of ___(6)___ may lead to the production of ___(7)___.'

2 a) What are the main sources of air pollution?
  b) Make a table showing:
  (i) the substances which cause air pollution,
  (ii) the damage which each of these substances can cause,
  (iii) the methods used to prevent pollution from each of these substances.

3 Get into a group with two or three others. Discuss the following questions.
  a) What further steps should be taken to reduce air pollution in industrial areas?
  b) Why do you think the Government does *not* introduce stricter controls over air pollution?

6 Environment or exploitation

In 1989, work started on the construction of a huge new coal mine near Asfordby in Leicestershire. The mine is below some of the most beautiful countryside and the richest farmland in England (figure 1). Eventually, the mine will produce about 4 million tonnes of coal every year.

Can we exploit raw materials, like coal, and yet preserve beautiful countryside like this in Leicestershire?

The Asfordby mine, built in 1989

Figure 1

Before work started on the mine, a public enquiry was held. People involved in the project, and others affected by it, expressed their views and concerns. The main arguments in the public enquiry are summarised in figure 2.

About 5000 people are unemployed in the area. The mine will create hundreds of new jobs. The extra traffic, noise and dust will be strictly controlled

Mr. Mine Manager

The mine will provide about 4 million tonnes of good quality low cost coal each year for 40 years. Costs will be competitive with foreign imports. There are now cleaner ways of using coal. Until alternative energy sources are found, coal is safer than nuclear fuel

Miss Politician

The mine will spoil beautiful countryside. Our pretty, peaceful villages will be ruined. Traffic noise and congestion on country lanes will be terrible

Mrs. Resident

Figure 2 Should we have coal mines in areas of natural beauty?

Notice how there were points 'for' and 'against' the plans for the coal mine. This is what we should expect. Whenever we develop large quarries and mines to exploit the Earth's raw materials, there are certain to be positive and negative effects.

Notice how the views that people express can be divided into four different issues.

■ **Social issues:** for example,
will it provide employment,
will it cause a strain on present community services?

■ **Environmental issues:** for example,
will it damage the countryside with roads, large buildings, etc.,
will it produce dust and pollution?

■ **Financial issues:** for example,
what is the cost of the raw material,
will it provide profits for investors?

■ **Location issues** related to where the mine is sited: for example, are the present roads in the area adequate for more traffic?

Things to do

1 Look at the views expressed in figure 2.
  a) Make a list of all the points in favour of the mine.
  b) Make a list of all the points against the mine.
  c) Write the letter 'S' by all the points in your lists which relate to social issues. Then, put the letter 'E' against points related to environmental issues, 'F' against financial issues and 'L' against location issues.
  d) What are your views about the development of the mine at Asfordby?

2 Suppose there are plans to develop a large waste tip near your home. A public meeting is arranged to discuss the plans. Some people will be in favour and others will be against the proposal.
Write down what each of the following people might say at the meeting about one important point. Choose a different point for each person:
(i)   The secretary of the local house owners' association.
(ii) The manager of a local waste disposal firm.
(iii) A representative of the local trade unions.
(iv) The local MP.

7 Using the land

About one-third of the Earth's surface is land. The other two-thirds are covered by water. Land is one of our most important resources. We live on it, we build our homes on it and grow our food on it. Because of this, we need to take care over the way we use it. Unfortunately, there are conflicts about the way in which we use the land.

These photos will give you some idea of the conflicts which arise in our use of the environment. What conflicts do they show?

Usually we have to balance the advantages and the disadvantages in the way we use the land. We all need homes to live in but rows of houses are less attractive than green fields. Building can also destroy the habitats of animals and plants. We need energy for our homes, vehicles and industries, but power stations, oil refineries and coal mines are often unsightly. We need minerals and materials for building, but quarries and gravel pits are ugly scars creating noise and dirt. Fortunately, there are strict laws in Britain to prevent people changing the use of their land just as they please. These are called Town and Country Planning Acts. There are similar laws in other industrialised countries, but not in parts of Eastern Europe or in the undeveloped countries of Africa, Asia and South America.

When the environment has been damaged, it is sometimes possible to restore it after use. Two examples of this are shown in the photos on the right.

So many walkers use the Pennine Way that the ground has begun to erode. Here the path is being built up to repair the damage and to stop further erosion

The International Festival Gardens in Liverpool are built on a waste tip

Things to do

1 Today, people in the UK have more leisure time and are more able to travel than ever before. This puts pressure on our roads and on those areas that we use for leisure. We have problems of conserving the countryside and, at the same time, trying to provide for its use and enjoyment. The map of the UK shows the major urban areas, major motorways, National Parks and Areas of Outstanding Natural Beauty.

a) Make a copy of the map. On your copy:
(i) name the major urban areas,
(ii) name the ten National Parks,
(iii) mark the following motorways: M1, M4, M25, M6.

b) Which of the National Parks or Areas of Outstanding Natural Beauty have you visited?

c) Do you think we should have more National Parks or Areas of Outstanding Natural Beauty? Explain your answer. If you say 'Yes', write down where you think these should be.

2 Get into a small group with two or three others. Discuss the following questions.

a) Are local councils and the Government in the best position to make laws to control our use of land?

- major urban areas
- motorways
- National Parks
- Areas of Outstanding Natural Beauty and forest parks

b) Do you think there should be stricter laws to control our use of land?

c) What are the points for and against stricter laws?

15

A few centuries ago, our ancestors could get around no faster than their legs (or the legs of their animals) could carry them. To build their homes, their castles, their churches and bridges, they had nothing more than their own strength and simple tools. Their weapons were also fairly crude – catapults, swords, bows and arrows.

All this has now changed. We can travel half way round the world in a few hours. We have powerful tools and machines for quarrying, mining, building and road making. Sadly, our weapons are those of devastation and mass destruction.

The Earth is about 400 thousand million years old. Our first ancestors evolved about 250 thousand years ago. So, for thousands of years, the impact of humans on the Earth was relatively small and the human population grew very slowly (figure 1).

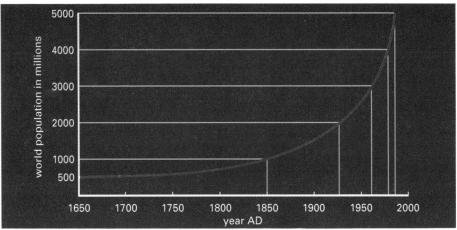

Figure 1

Notice in figure 1 how fast the human population has grown since 1850. During this time, our impact on the Earth has become greater and greater. Our machines, our technology and our weapons are now so powerful that they can destroy us.

Since the Industrial Revolution in the nineteenth century, we have developed larger and larger tools, more powerful machines and deadlier weapons.

Oil spills during the Gulf War in 1991 killed thousands of sea birds and polluted huge areas of sea and coastline

Pollution from burning oil wells in Kuwait during the Gulf War reached areas as far away as Russia and India

During the last century, improved hygiene, better diets and increased medical care have enabled people to live longer. At the same time, the birth rate has increased because there are more healthy men and women able to reproduce. These factors have brought about a rapid increase in the world population since 1850.

Our impact on the Earth is largely due to the increasing human population. More and more people need more food, more water and more space. This means we require more land for farming and for industries. At the same time, we take more of the Earth's resources and we create more pollution.

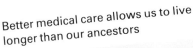

Better medical care allows us to live longer than our ancestors

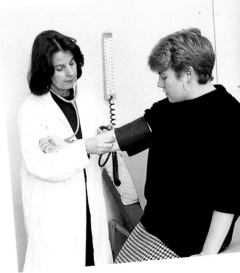

Most people eat a better diet and are more healthy than 100 years ago

Things to do

1 Look at the graphs below showing the world use of coal and oil and the world production of aluminium during the twentieth century.

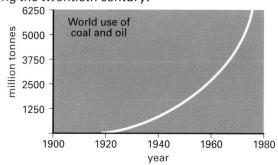

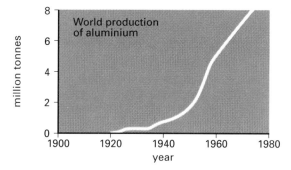

a) How long did it take the world use of coal and oil
   (i) to double from 1250 to 2500 million tonnes,
   (ii) to double from 2500 to 5000 million tonnes?
b) How long did it take the world production of aluminium
   (i) to double from 2 to 4 million tonnes,
   (ii) to double from 4 to 8 million tonnes?
c) Look at figure 1. How long did it take the human population to double from 2000 to 4000 millions?
d) Why do you think your answers to (a) and (b) are shorter than your answer to (c)?
e) Most people think that the population explosion cannot go on forever. What do you think? What factors might limit the growth of the world's population?
f) What steps do you think should be taken to control the population explosion?

2 Leroy thinks that all the major catastrophes throughout the world can be related to the population explosion. Liz does not think that any major catastrophes are related to the population explosion. Do you agree with Leroy or Liz, or do you have your own opinion? Explain your view and give examples.

In Britain, we use about 20 000 million litres of water every day. This would not be a problem if we all used water carefully and sensibly, but we don't. In cities and industrial areas, waste water is often pumped straight into rivers or into the sea. Usually, fish are the first to be affected by polluted water. Then, plants begin to die and eventually only algae can survive. By this stage, it is too dangerous to swim in the water, never mind drink it.

Sewage

Sewage is the main cause of water pollution. Each day Thames Water Authority treats 950 million gallons of sewage. But in some towns, the sewage is dumped straight into rivers with little or no treatment. Bacteria feed on this sewage and grow so fast that all the oxygen in the water is used up. Fish and water plants therefore die and the river becomes a stinking sewer.

Hot water

Hot water is pumped into rivers from power stations where it has been used for cooling. This may seem harmless, but hot water dissolves less oxygen than cold water. This affects fish in particular, which are adapted to live in cold water containing a higher concentration of dissolved oxygen.

What causes water pollution?

Chemicals

Chemicals from factories often cause water pollution. Poisonous industrial wastes include lead compounds used in petrol, mercury from factories producing chlorine, and oil from tankers and refineries. Pollution caused by major oil slicks, such as those in Alaska and the Gulf, has been very bad in recent years. In Britain it is illegal for any industry to dump its waste into our rivers or the sea without the consent of their water authority.

Fertilisers

Fertilisers are spread on the land and can get into rivers and streams. If this happens, fertilisers have a similar effect to sewage. They cause bacteria to grow so fast that all the oxygen in the water is used up and other living things die.

In poorer countries of the Third World, ten million children die every year from diseases caused by polluted water. These diseases include cholera, typhoid and dysentry. These sad facts show us how important it is to have clean water. They also explain the importance of checking any processes which might have an effect on the purity of the water.

Everyone should have clean water for drinking and washing

Things to do

1 The diagram below shows a ten mile stretch of a river. The numbered arrows show where pollution enters the river. For each of the arrows say what type of pollution is involved.

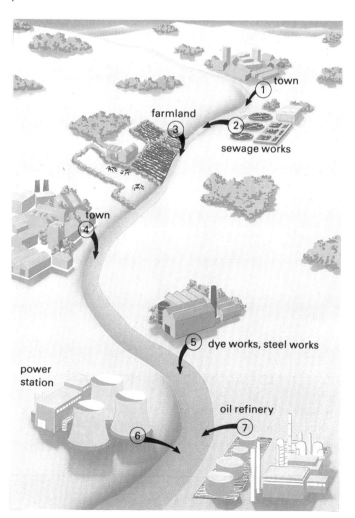

2 Ask your teacher to help you to check a river or a stream for water pollution.

a) Look at the river and its banks carefully.

(i) Can you see any river animals (e.g. ducks, moorhen, frogs, fish)?

(ii) Are there insects on, or in, the water?

(iii) Are there plenty of weeds along the river bank?

(iv) Is the water surface clean and free from scum?

(v) Is there any rotting material or waste in the water?

(vi) Is the water clear?

b) Take a sample of the river water.

(i) How clear is the water compared to tap water?

(ii) Test the pH of the water. (Pure water should have a pH close to 7.)

c) Prepare a short report of your survey.

3 a) Why is the amount of dissolved oxygen important in keeping a river clean?

b) How is the amount of dissolved oxygen in river water affected by:

(i) fertilisers, (ii) hot water?

c) What happens when the amount of dissolved oxygen in a river falls sharply?

19

10 Water supply and sewage

Supplying clean water to our homes and factories

Each one of us in the UK uses about 150 litres of water every day. Most of the water supplied to our homes is used for baths, for washing or for flushing the lavatory.

Most of our water in the UK comes from rivers, lakes or underground wells. But, before we use the water, it must be checked, treated and purified so that it is safe to drink. Figure 1 shows the main stages in water treatment.

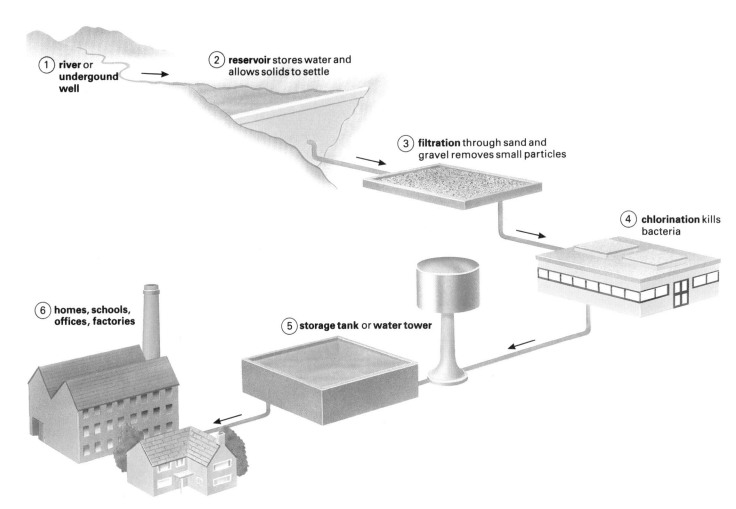

1 **river** or **undergound well**

2 **reservoir** stores water and allows solids to settle

3 **filtration** through sand and gravel removes small particles

4 **chlorination** kills bacteria

5 **storage tank** or **water tower**

6 **homes, schools, offices, factories**

Figure 1 Water treatment

Treating water after it has been used

The work of water authorities in supplying clean water is only half of the story. After clean water has been used, it is called **sewage**. Sewage is water mixed with waste material such as bits of food, detergents, urine and faeces. This sewage must be cleaned and purified before it is returned to rivers or they will become polluted. In some areas, the water from a river may be used two or three times in homes and factories before it eventually reaches the sea.

Figure 2 shows the main stages at a sewage works.

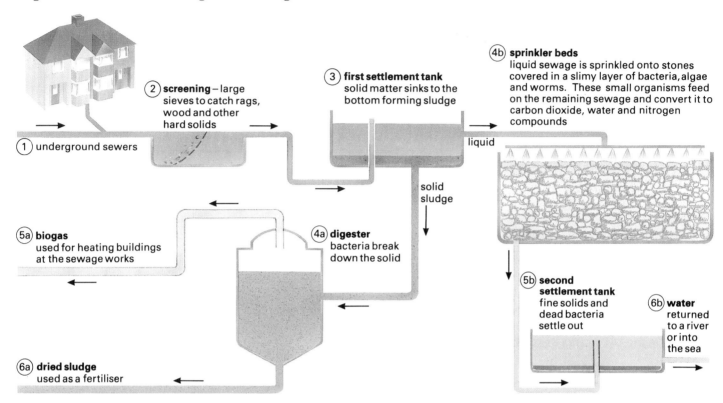

Figure 2 Sewage treatment

Things to do

1 a) Use figure 1 to draw a flow chart of the stages that water goes through before it is used in our homes and factories. Use only one or two words to summarise each stage.

b) Use figure 2 to draw a similar flow chart for sewage treatment.

2 The Water Services bill posted to Mr Chadwick is shown on the right.

a) How does the cost of the water supply compare with the cost of sewerage services?

b) Mr Chadwick lives with his wife and 14-year-old daughter. They each use about 150 litres of water every day.

   (i)   How much water does the Chadwick family use every day?

   (ii)   How much water does the Chadwick family use in one year?

   (iii) How much does the family pay for water services in one year?

   (iv) How much does the family pay per litre of water for water services?

   (v)   How does the cost of 1 litre of water compare with the cost of 1 litre of milk?

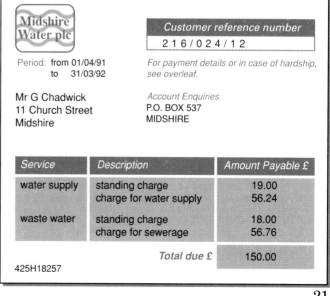

Midshire Water plc

Customer reference number
2 1 6 / 0 2 4 / 1 2

Period: from 01/04/91
      to   31/03/92

For payment details or in case of hardship, see overleaf.

Mr G Chadwick
11 Church Street
Midshire

Account Enquiries
P.O. BOX 537
MIDSHIRE

Service	Description	Amount Payable £
water supply	standing charge	19.00
	charge for water supply	56.24
waste water	standing charge	18.00
	charge for sewerage	56.76
	Total due £	150.00

425H18257

Activities

1 Acid rain in Norway and Sweden

Scientists in Norway and Sweden have tried to track down the sources of their acid rain. The results of their work are shown in the diagram.

a) What percentage of the acid rain comes from inside Norway and Sweden?

b) What percentage of the acid rain falling on Norway and Sweden is *not* accounted for in the diagram?

c) Which six countries are the worst in causing acid rain in Norway and Sweden?

d) Make a bar chart showing these six countries and the percentages of the acid rain which they cause.

e) Air pollution from industries is worse in Poland than in the UK and Poland is nearer Norway and Sweden. Yet Poland causes much less acid rain than the UK in Norway and Sweden. Why is this?

f) Draw a flow diagram to show how sulphur in coal used in the UK causes acid rain in Norway.

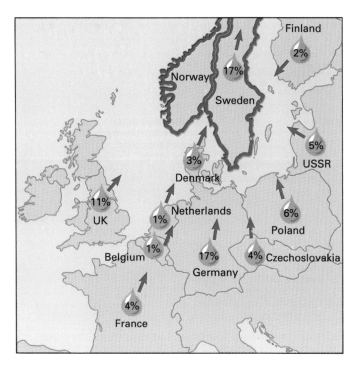

The source of acid rain in Norway and Sweden

2 Traffic noise

Get into a small group with two or three other students. Imagine that you are a family that lives on a very busy road. At times, the traffic noise is very unpleasant. Discuss the following questions.

a) Is noise a form of pollution?

b) How could you cut down the traffic noise in your garden?

c) How could you cut down the traffic noise when you are indoors?

d) What steps could be taken to reduce traffic noise in towns and cities?

e) Design a poster with a slogan to try to persuade motorcyclists to make less noise.

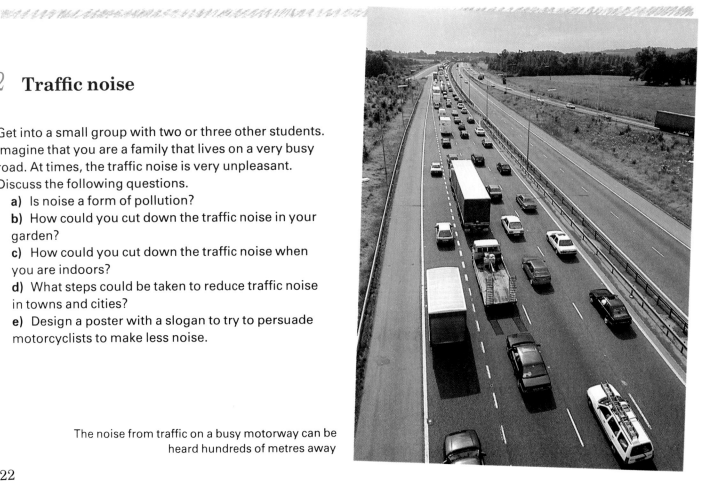

The noise from traffic on a busy motorway can be heard hundreds of metres away

3 The water cycle

In the diagram and the passage below numbers have been used to show missing words. Which of the words in the box below can be used to replace each number?

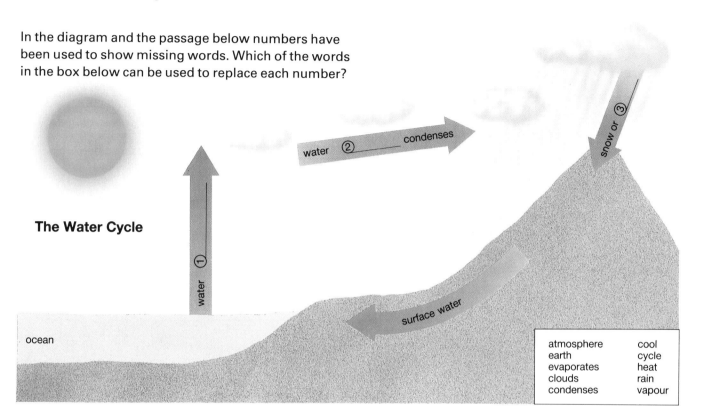

The Water Cycle

water ②   condenses

snow or ③

water ①

ocean

surface water

atmosphere	cool
earth	cycle
evaporates	heat
clouds	rain
condenses	vapour

_____(4)_____ from the sun causes water to evaporate into the ___(5)___ from rivers, lakes and oceans. This water vapour rises and forms ___(6)___ . As the clouds rise, they ___(7)___ and the water vapour ___(8)___ to form drops of water. These fall back to the earth as rain which soaks into the ___(9)___ or joins rivers and oceans. The whole ___(10)___ then begins again.

4 Smoking and your health

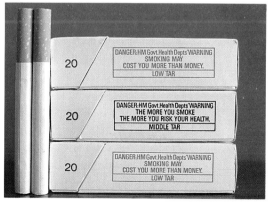

Discuss the following questions in groups of 3 or 4.
  a) In which ways can smoking damage your health?
  b) In which ways can smoking pollute a room and the people in it?
  c) Why do you think some teenagers take up smoking?

  d) What further steps should be taken to make teenagers more aware of the dangers of smoking?
  e) Prepare a report of your discussions (about 250 words) for the rest of your class.

5 Recycling aluminium

At present, there is enough aluminium ore to provide all the aluminium we need for about 30 years. Because of this, more and more aluminium is being recycled.

Most of us waste aluminium by throwing away milk bottle tops and foil. In this activity, you can estimate how much aluminium could be recycled from bottle tops and foil.

a) Estimate the number of milk bottle tops your family uses each week.

b) Estimate the area of aluminium foil (in square centimetres) which your family uses each week.

c) Use your answers in (a) and (b) to work out the mass of aluminium your family uses each week.
Assume: 1 milk bottle top weighs 0.2 g
100 cm^2 of foil weighs 0.5 g

d) If possible, collect results from the rest of your class. Find an average value for the mass of aluminium used per family in one week.

e) Estimate the amount of aluminium in your survey which gets recycled. Do any of the families in your survey save aluminium for recycling?

At this plant, aluminium cans are separated from steel cans and compressed into slabs ready for recycling

f) Estimate the number of families in the UK. (The population of the UK is 55 million.)

g) Use your answers to (d) and (f) to estimate the total mass of aluminium bottle tops and foil used in the UK:
(i) in one week,
(ii) in one year.

h) About 35% of aluminium used in the UK is recycled. What difficulties are there in trying to recycle more?

i) Which forms of aluminium do you think are easiest to recycle?

6 Catalytic converters

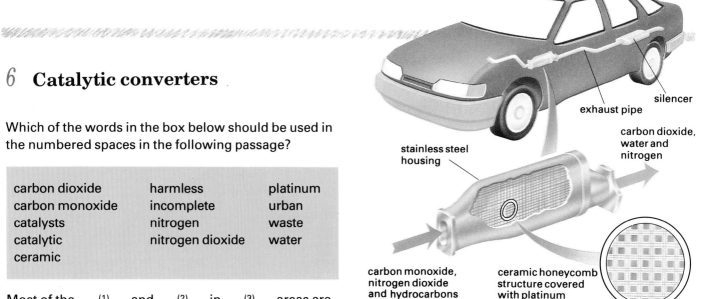

silencer
exhaust pipe
carbon dioxide, water and nitrogen
stainless steel housing
carbon monoxide, nitrogen dioxide and hydrocarbons
A catalytic converter
ceramic honeycomb structure covered with platinum and rhodium

Which of the words in the box below should be used in the numbered spaces in the following passage?

carbon dioxide	harmless	platinum
carbon monoxide	incomplete	urban
catalysts	nitrogen	waste
catalytic	nitrogen dioxide	water
ceramic		

Most of the ___(1)___ and ___(2)___ in ___(3)___ areas are produced by the ___(4)___ combustion of petrol in car engines. Up to 90% of these gases could be removed if all cars were fitted with ___(5)___ converters (see diagram).

As the ___(6)___ gases pass out through the exhaust pipe, they are forced through the converter. This has a honeycomb structure of ___(7)___ material which is coated with a thin layer of ___(8)___ and rhodium alloy. These metals act as ___(9)___. They convert carbon monoxide in the exhaust gases into ___(10)___, hydrocarbons into carbon dioxide, and ___(11)___ and nitrogen dioxide into ___(12)___. This makes the exhaust gases ___(13)___.

7 Compost from household waste

The diagram below shows one method of using household waste.

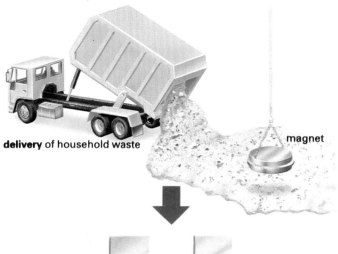

delivery of household waste   **magnet**

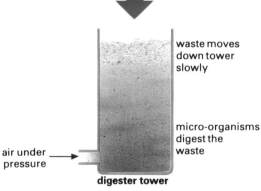

shredder cuts material into pieces about 10 cm in diameter

waste moves down tower slowly

micro-organisms digest the waste

air under pressure →

digester tower

compost crushed and bagged for sale

COMPOST

a) Draw a flow diagram to summarise the process in the diagram on the left.

b) What types of material might be found in the household waste?

c) (i) Name the material removed by the magnet.
(ii) What will this be used for?

d) What other materials should be removed before shredding the waste?

e) Why is it necessary to shred the household waste?

f) Why is air blown into the digester tower?

Costing compost

A small firm operates a waste disposal plant similar to the one shown in the diagram above.
The main costs to the firm are:

Wages:	Helen (part-time secretary)	£50 per week
	Jeff (manager/driver)	£200 per week
	Greg (plant operator)	£150 per week
Hire of lorry		£100 per week
Running costs, repair and **payment** for disposal plant		£100 per week
Other costs		£150 per week

g) Suggest four items in the firm's 'other costs' of £150 per week.

h) What are the firm's total costs per week?

i) The waste plant has five digester towers. Each produces 2 tonnes of compost per week. This is sold to garden centres in bags containing 50 kg of compost (1 tonne = 1000 kg).

(i) How many bags of compost does the firm produce each week?

(ii) For how much should the firm sell each bag of compost in order to recover its costs?

8 Burning stubble

Many people have complained about farmers burning off waste straw and stubble. This has led to laws controlling the burning of stubble.

a) What is stubble?

b) Is stubble biodegradable?

c) Why do farmers burn stubble?

d) What problems and hazards are caused by burning stubble?

e) How could the problems and hazards be kept to a minimum?

f) What other possible uses are there for stubble and waste straw?

9 Studying lichens

Farheen and Jamie decided to study lichens in their own village near Birmingham and also when they were on holiday in Snowdonia. In each place, they chose a sandstone wall facing west. First, they looked for the different types of lichen on the walls. Then, they chose ten lichens at random and measured their diameters. Finally, they measured the edge to edge distance from each of these ten lichens to its nearest neighbour. This provides a measure of the density of lichens on each wall.

Here are their results:

Home survey (near Birmingham)

Types of lichen	Lichen diam. /mm	Distance to nearest lichen/mm
green powder lichen	18	104
	24	97
	7	84
grey crust lichen	4	105
	34	76
	21	28
	14	63
	7	164
	31	82
	8	36

Snowdonia survey

Types of lichen	Lichen diam. /mm	Distance to nearest lichen/mm
green powder lichen	5	15
grey crust lichen	65	9
bordered wall lichen	50	8
	25	27
common orange lichen	46	0
	9	32
puffed shield lichen	30	12
	47	5
	53	16
	14	23

a) Calculate the average diameter of lichen at the two sites.

b) Calculate the average distance to the nearest lichen at the two sites.

c) How do the number of types of lichen, lichen size and lichen density vary from one site to the other?

d) Why do you think the types, the size and the density of lichens vary from one site to the other?

e) What further tests could Farheen and Jamie carry out to check whether the suggestions in part d) are possible?

10 Using our waste

Figure 1 shows one method of making use of
biodegradable household waste.

The household waste is first compressed so that there
are no pockets of air in it. It is then put into a large hole
lined with plastic. The waste is now called biomass. It
slowly breaks down producing biogas which contains
methane.

a) Give three examples of household waste that can
be used in this process.
b) Which organisms cause the breakdown of the
waste?
c) Name one other gas that is present in biogas
besides methane.
d) Why do you think the waste is first compressed
so that there are no air pockets in it?

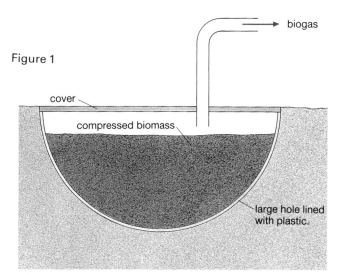

Figure 1

e) Why do you think the hole is lined with plastic?
f) What could the biogas be used for?
g) Suppose the residents association in your area
are planning to build a plant like the one in figure 1.
Write a letter to their secretary giving the points 'for'
and 'against' their proposal.

11 Sewage outflow

The diagram below shows the position of a sewage
outflow pipe on a beach.

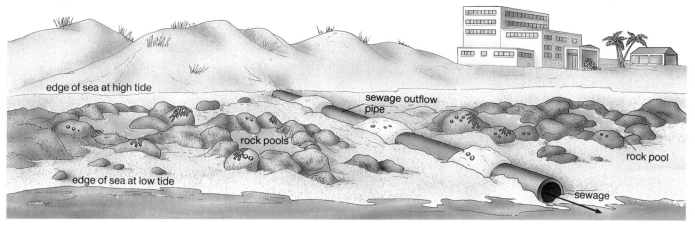

The whole beach is covered in different seaweeds,
growing on rocks and in rock pools. The main species
of animal in and around the rock pools are crabs,
mussels, barnacles, limpets and fish.

There is concern that the animals and plants are being
affected by the sewage from the pipe.

You and a group of friends have been asked to
investigate the situation.

a) How would you measure the size of the
population of one of the animals in the study area
near the sewage pipe?
b) How would you compare the seaweeds growing
in the study area on this beach with those growing
on a beach where there was no sewage pipe?
c) Suggest three factors, other than the presence of
the sewage pipe, which could affect the types of
plants and animals found on the two beaches.

12 Sandwell and gravel

Sandwell is a small country village about 20 miles south of Bristol. The village is surrounded by rich farm land and there is a small nature reserve nearby. The nature reserve has some rare butterflies and plants.

Bollom's Gravel Company own marshland between Sandwell and the nature reserve. This marshland could provide thousands of tonnes of sand and gravel over a period of several years. Bollom's Gravel Company say that the proposed gravel pit will cause little environmental damage. They also say that it will bring many benefits to the village. Once the gravel has been removed, Bollom's have said they will redevelop the site as an area of natural beauty.

The villagers of Sandwell do not agree with Bollom's Gravel Company. They think that the gravel pit will cause a lot of environmental damage and change their way of life. A committee of local people has been set up to oppose the gravel company.

a) Give three ways in which sand or gravel from the gravel pit might be used.

b) How might the proposed gravel pit benefit the people in Sandwell?

c) How may the village life in Sandwell be less pleasant if work is started on the gravel pit?

d) How might a gravel pit affect the wildlife in the area?

e) How could the site be redeveloped as an area of natural beauty when all the gravel has been removed?

f) Suppose a public meeting has been arranged to hear the arguments for and against the gravel pit. Various people have been asked to read out statements at the public meeting. These statements should be no more than 300 words. Write down what you would say in your statement if you were:

   (i)   the manager of Bollom's Gravel Company,
   (ii) the chairman of the local committee in Sandwell.

A working gravel pit like this one in Gloucestershire can certainly have a huge impact on the local landscape and scenery

The Silkworth Colliery in Sunderland was flooded and landscaped when work stopped there. Now it provides open parkland and lakes for local people to enjoy

13 Steel for Tollun

Tollun is an island of a developing country. Its main exports are fish, maize and soft fruit. It also has a flourishing tourist industry.

The Government is keen to improve road links, increase exports, build hotels and expand the tourist trade. As part of these plans, it has asked the Eurosteel Company to build an iron and steel works on the island.

Large deposits of iron pyrites are found on the island. When iron is obtained from this ore, sulphur dioxide is formed. There are also good deposits of limestone and coal for the iron making process.

The map of Tollun below shows the main towns, roads and important areas. **W**, **X**, **Y** and **Z** are possible sites for the iron and steel works.

a) Make a list of the advantages and disadvantages for each of the four sites.

b) Which of the four sites would you recommend the Tollun Government to use? Give the main reasons for your choice.

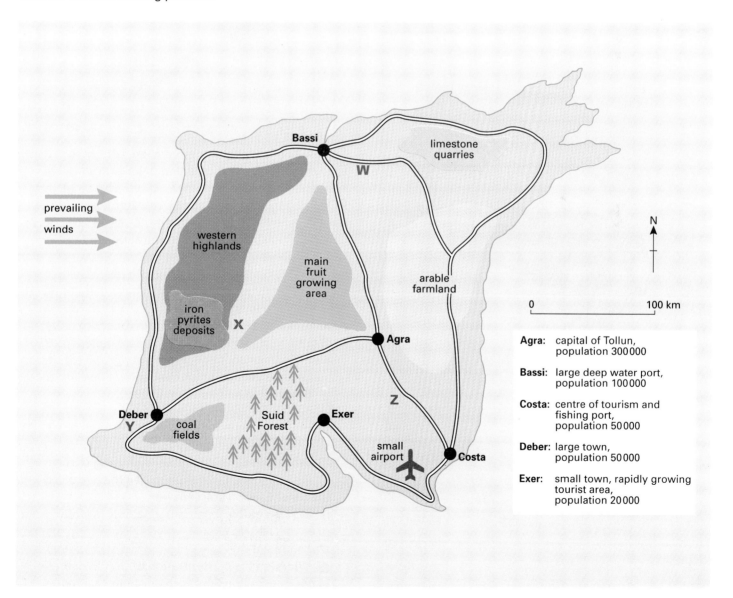

Agra: capital of Tollun, population 300000

Bassi: large deep water port, population 100000

Costa: centre of tourism and fishing port, population 50000

Deber: large town, population 50000

Exer: small town, rapidly growing tourist area, population 20000

14 Ospreys

Ospreys are sometimes called fish eagles. They are large birds of prey which eat mainly fish. Scientists have been studying the breeding colonies of ospreys in the Long Island area of the USA since 1950. The table below shows the number of breeding pairs in the area between 1950 and 1980.

Year	1950	1955	1960	1965	1970	1975	1980
Number of breeding pairs	1000	540	380	190	100	120	180

An Osprey ripping into its catch

The food chain below shows the ospreys' main source of food.

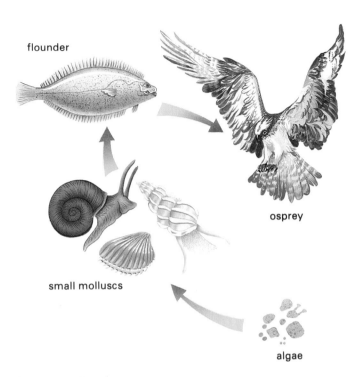

flounder

osprey

small molluscs

algae

Scientists found that the insecticide, DDT, was causing the fall in numbers of breeding pairs of birds. It was being used to kill mosquitoes. After being used, the DDT got into river water and sea water. Very soon it was detected in algae, then in molluscs, in flounders and later in ospreys. The concentrations of DDT in some ospreys were about one million times more than in algae. The use of DDT was eventually banned.

a) What advantage do ospreys have in building their nests on an island?

b) Plot a graph of the number of breeding pairs of osprey (vertically) against the years between 1950 and 1980 (horizontally). From your graph estimate:
   (i)   the year in which the osprey population dropped to half its value in 1950,
   (ii) the number of breeding pairs in 1962,
   (iii) the year in which people stopped using DDT.

c) What are the advantages of using DDT?

d) What are the disadvantages of using DDT?

e) Do you think it was right to ban the use of DDT in the area? Explain your answer.

f) DDT is soluble in fat, but insoluble in water. How does this help to explain why DDT builds up in plants and animals?

g) Why was the concentration of DDT in ospreys about one million times greater than in algae?

15 Pollution in the River Whit

The map below shows an area on either side of the River Whit on the north-west side of Whitvale. Local people have complained that the river is polluted and the river authority has discovered a high level of nitrates in the river at X.

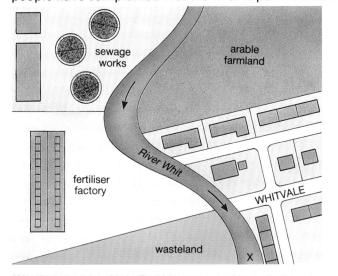

a) Suggest three possible sources of the nitrate pollution at X.
b) For each of these sources:
 (i) say how the level of nitrate pollution will vary with the seasons of the year,
(ii) explain why the variation occurs.
c) What effects will the nitrate pollution cause in the river?
d) Explain why the nitrate pollution has these effects.
e) Write a plan to investigate where the nitrate pollution is coming from. (You do not need to describe any chemical tests for nitrates.)

16 Checking river pollution

The map below shows a river system which ends at the sea. Letters on the map show the level of water pollution at different points in the river system.

A indicates no pollution, B indicates low pollution, C shows high pollution and D very high pollution.

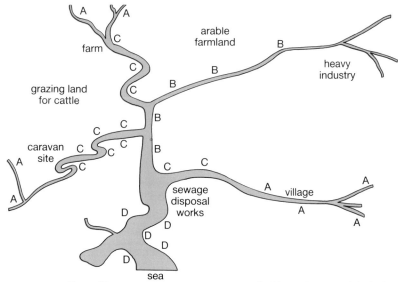

a) Where is the river most polluted?
b) Why is the river most polluted here?
c) What evidence is there that the farm and caravan site are polluting the river?
d) In which way do you think the farm pollutes the river water?

e) How do you think the water pollution will vary at different times of the year?
f) What steps could be taken to reduce the water pollution throughout the whole river system?

17 Water purity

dye works

ALLCOLOUR DYE CO

overflow pipe

B

Flow of River Churl

A

Harminder Ali is an Environmental Health Officer. He took samples of water from the River Churl just before and just after the outflow pipe from Allcolour Dye Company.

Harminder found that the water from point **A** had a pH of 7.0, while that from **B** had a pH of 2.0.

a) How has the water changed between A and B?

b) What do you think has caused the change?

Substance	Mass of substance which dissolves in 100 cm³ of water at 10°C	pH of saturated solution
calcium hydroxide	0.13 g	12.0
magnesium hydroxide	0.07 g	9.3
sodium hydroxide	102.00 g	14.0

Local environmental health regulations say that the waste water from factories must have a pH between 7.5 and 9.5. The table on the left shows three alkaline substances that could be used to treat the waste water from Allcolour Dye Company.

c) Which is the most soluble of the three alkaline substances and what is the pH of its saturated solution?

d) What would be the effect of adding too much calcium hydroxide?

e) Which substance should Harminder Ali choose to treat the waste water? Explain your choice.

f) Suppose you are provided with several litres of waste water from the Allcolour Dye Company and a supply of your chosen substance.
Describe how you would find out how much of the chosen substance is needed to increase the pH of 1 litre of the waste water to 8.0.